Hope

for

Hydro-
cephalus
by: Terra Robinson

Dedication

Hope for Hydro is dedicated to the miracle doctors, Dr. Parent and Dr. Graves, their staff, and the other medical staff. My cousins in Jackson, MS-Dee, Sean, and Stan.

My loving family:
Husband-Dwayne Robinson

Our beautiful children-Tyerria (my miracle superhero), Luxury, Lysanius, Chelisa, Mariah

My brothers Kelly, Marvin, Gary, Arthur, and Timothy

Sisters- Jeanette and Willyne-my other two heartbeats-Love you guys dearly.

Most importantly, my two deceased sisters-Joyce and Renee were fun-loving, spirited-filled, and full of love and laughter. You two are truly missed and will forever live within us.

My in-laws-Glenda, C.J. Harris, and my sisters-n-brothers-in-law

Last, my book is dedicated to my deceased parents, Arthur and Cora Wordlaw. Life is not the same, but your legacy lives on! Love you guys!

Contents

Foreword

In writing this book, my entire focus was to create a book that talks about the miracle of birth that brings about the joy and blessing of being a parent to an amazing daughter (children). Although the text is brief, it explains the in-depth complications of birth with the shocking disability brought to the surface. I am sharing the intimacy of a young mother, wife, schoolteacher, and Pastor's wife, struggles of conceiving, intense labor, and the harsh diagnosis of my only child (at that time) having a disability called Hydrocephalus.

My vision (V'Zon) for this book, Hope for Hydro, is filled with pain and joy of coming to an understanding of what Hydrocephalus is, along with the struggles of having a career and (yes, I forgot) being a sergeant in the United States Army Reserves.

I hope you all receive love from this fantastic book and gain pleasure knowing your child can live a normal and blessed life with Hydrocephalus.

Terra Robinson

Preface

Hope for Hydro is a book encouraging all parents, especially parents of a "Water head baby," which is the nonmedical term for Hydrocephalus. This book will inspire you to feel the pain of learning about a disability that was never a part of my life, even as a schoolteacher of 25 years. I never heard of this medical condition before the birth of Tyerria. To encourage, God's blessing is greater than anything, and He presented me with a courageous daughter that was granted life through His mercy of giving her a great team of specialists, Doctors, and Therapists that wanted a normal life for Tyerria. This book provides hope for all mothers facing challenges, heartbreak, and obstacles that can be overcome with the blessing of Christ.

Acknowledgment

I am grateful to all that helped me in writing this book. I am grateful to Pamela Dankins for leading me on the path of helping me with the proper steps in getting my book into the publishing arena. I thank all my family and friends that encouraged me to keep writing and told me they could not wait to read this. I love you all, and I give you all special thanks. Last, I want to thank my husband, Pastor Dwayne Robinson, for being my biggest cheerleader and giving me encouragement when I felt like giving up. I love my family and thank God for you all.

One
HOPE FOR HEALTHY

Excitement! Joy! Hope! Love! Surprised! Shocked! Warmth!

Those emotions flowed through my mind when I found out I was pregnant. Why? Because it took me two long years to conceive, and I was at my ultimate breaking point. I tried and cried for so long, and it seemed hopeless.

Hopeless- not expecting good or success. www.Merriam-Webster.com

My friends were all either pregnant or had a child. I longed for my child, not because my friend had or expected a child, but because I had mapped out my life and even the time frame that I would start a family. See, I got married right out of high school and was 18 years old-went to the military-Army Reserve-started college-quit for the workforce- and wanted to give my high school sweetheart a token of our love by having a child. My brain told me that at 24 years, your family will start because you will already have an established career.

stopped, and I told my husband I wanted to start our family. We were both happy, and he could not wait to start.

We did everything to conceive by waiting on ovulation time, taking vitamins, and anything else that someone mentioned even took Geritol, one of the old wives' tales. Take two Geritol daily, and you can conceive a child within six months.

Ovulation- is the process that usually happens once in every menstrual cycle. When hormone changes, it triggers an ovary to release an egg to be fertilized by sperm. www.webmd.com

After a year, my husband Terry and I decided it was time to take a trip to the doctor. We want to know if anything is wrong with my body or his sperm count. We had heard that if the sperm count were too low, conceiving would be hard. We made an appointment. We went to the nearest women's clinic, talked to OGBYN (Obstetrician-gynecologist), and got blood work from us and sperm analysis.

Sperm Analysis- when the sperm count test analyzes the health and viability of a man's sperm. www.healthline.com After testing, the OBGYN showed us the proper way to count ovulation days and told us to stop worrying and take it one day at a time. He informed us that stress causes more harm because it takes away the enjoyment of wanting to conceive. Sex becomes a chore to conceive. He advised us on healthy foods that could help us conceive, such as leafy vegetables, greens, fortified cereals, oranges, strawberries, and beans (**www.whattoexpect.com**).

We thanked the doctor and left without saying a word to each other. At home, we tried to stick with a healthy diet and the pleasures of having sex to conceive without unwanted stress, but it was hard. We tried to return life to normal by hanging out with friends and family. We were both working hard and pushing the thoughts of having a baby in the back of our minds. However, during the next six months, I did something different. I prayed. I prayed to God and reminded him of the Scriptures-Ask and shall be given unto you (Matthew 7:7-8. paraphrased). God will provide you with the desire of your heart. I know it is not like God does not know already, but I want it to remind him of His Words, which I needed Him to fulfill.

Two
HOPE FOR PREGNANCY

Oh, God! What's happening? I'm Sick to my Stomach!
Sorry! I Couldn't Make it to the Toilet!
Vomit Everywhere!

One morning in September. I woke up with this funny feeling in my stomach. It was in 1998. My husband asked me what was wrong. I thought we were sleeping in today. It is only eight o'clock. Go back to sleep. I could not. I rushed to the bathroom but did not make it. I vomited everywhere, all over the floor and in Terry's shoes. I apologized many times, and he got up and helped me clean up the mess. He even went to the kitchen and brought back baking powder and water.

Baking Powder water is the old family recipe to help settle the stomach.

After a few minutes, I felt fine, so I cooked. This feeling came again, and I lost it. I started throwing up again. So immediately, Terry took me to our family clinic, Dr. Simmons. She was open on Saturdays from 8:00 A.M. to 12:00 P.M. When we arrived, it was not a long wait. We went in, and I explained my symptoms, and she did some blood work. As we waited, I told Terry that it had to be something I ate. About 15 minutes later, she congratulated us and told us I was pregnant. It was morning sickness.

Morning sickness- nausea and vomiting that occurs during pregnancy. www.mayoclinic.org

We were so excited and could not wait to tell the news. It took us two years to get pregnant. When we got home, I walked immediately to my mother's house. My sister Renee was sitting on the couch. I told her, "Guess what?" She said, "What?" I started laughing, and she got mad at me. So, I told her I was pregnant. Pregnant? She started laughing and said, "Yeah, I'm glad! You got that because you laughed at me when I was pregnant!" We started laughing, and then my mother walked in, and Renee blurted out that I was pregnant. My mother laughed and said, "Oh, I'm so happy and about time. I'm going to be a grandmother again." She got on the phone and called my other sisters and brothers. Some cousins and her sisters as well. It seemed like she wanted to call everyone to the latest gossip. After her 1000 phone calls, I told her I couldn't stop throwing up and had just returned from the doctor. She told me it would stop soon, but I needed to eat healthier from here on out because she knew how much I love potato chips. She said I had to eat vegetables, not for me, but for the baby. I laughed and told her to stop because I was feeling sick again. However, I promised I would eat better. I left my mother's house and returned to pick up my prenatal vitamins, some medicine for nausea, and some iron pills.

After I got my medicine, we went to his mother's house to tell her the news. However, his mother was not as thrilled as my mother and told us she would not babysit. She told me she isn't the grandmother that keeps children. These words hurt Terry and my feelings so severely that we just stood up and left. She told us to come back, but we were disappointed, and I told Terry that I would never ask her to babysit my child. He agreed. (However, she was there throughout the pregnancy, every baby shower, and mostly every visit, so I can honestly say she did not mean those words). It was about a week when my OGBYN appointment came. I had been taking my vitamins but was sick a lot. I could not keep much food down. My gynecologist was Dr. Will Locke, one of the most highly recommended doctors around Starkville knew I was losing weight instead of gaining, so he told me to take Flintstones vitamins and to ensure I took my iron pills. Dr. Locke took blood, urine samples, and a pelvic exam to ensure everything was all right and confirmed my pregnancy. He scheduled another doctor's appointment about a month out and gave me some brochures, some pamphlets on pregnancy, and a list of things to do and eat. Dr. Locke told me everything looked good and that my pelvis and cervix were strong and healthy. He assured us that the morning sickness would pass soon. Our first appointment finished, and we thanked him and went out of the clinic about our day.

For the next few months, I ate healthier by eating more vegetables, which I hated, but I knew I had to eat to have a healthy baby. Each doctor's visit was fine, and I was in a normal range of where I needed to be each month. In my third month, we had an ultrasound and heard the baby's heartbeat.

Ultrasound is an imaging test that uses sound waves to create a picture (a sonogram) of the body's organs, tissues, and other structures. https://med lineplus.gov/lab-tests/sonogram/

While looking at the screen, Dr. Locke told us we were having a boy but stated that it might be too early to say. Terry was as happy as he could be because he wanted a boy. It didn't matter to me because I only wanted a healthy baby. At the beginning of November, I got a back cold, and when I went to my appointment, Dr. Locke confirmed I had the flu, which I was not too fond of the flu. I was so weak and sick. I could only take Sudafed, which was not helping me. I remember going to Florida because my nephew was getting married. When we got to his house, I fell asleep on the couch, and all I could remember was that I was still on this couch the next day. I was so sweaty but felt better. He told me I missed the rehearsal dinner, and everybody went to the club and my sister's house. He said I was the unofficial babysitter, and I was glad the children were old enough to care for themselves because I couldn't move off the couch. That Saturday was the wedding, and we got up early Sunday morning, around 4 A.M., and headed back home.

Three
HOPE FOR THE BABY'S ROOM

Hopeful! Excited! Choose Nursery Colors! Shopping! I'M SOOOOO Happy!

We started decorating the baby's room around the seventh month of my pregnancy, which was 36 weeks. We chose the middle room as the baby's room, which we use as a spare bedroom. So, it was the perfect room for a nursery. We went shopping for furniture, but my mother told us to go layaway because we still had a few months. So, we bought a few baby clothes and other minor things. We got alphabet blocks to hang all over the first wall and put alphabet foam letters connecting mats on the floor. Also, we got a Disney mobile for the baby's crib. We chose a neutral color and decorated it with Mickey Mouse. Because I love Mickey Mouse, I had a Mickey Mouse comforter set and placed all kinds of stuffed animals in a crib. We put all the boys' clothes in the closet and looked at everything we had decorated. We set everything up in the baby's room. It was perfect. Later that evening, my mother surprised us with a baby shower at our house. Now I know why she wanted us to lay-away items. We received all kinds of gifts and were very grateful. My family and Terry's family were there.

We got everything we wanted and more. The baby had so many clothes, pampers, baby wipes, etc. We were so thankful, and we had so much food and gifts. We laughed and talked for a long time. Also, I was a teacher's assistant at Sudduth, and the Teachers, the assistants, and other staff members gave me a baby shower. So, we had tripled of stuff for the baby.

Can't wait until you arrive. Grandma Bo. Hi sweetie!

MMMM-That's go

My mother told me to come over that following Sunday because she had cooked a big breakfast. I told her I would be right over. I forgot to mention that I lived next door to my mother. So, I told my husband that Mom cooked breakfast for us. So, we got up, washed our faces, and brushed our teeth. By that time, I was hungry as ever. So, I went to open the door, and as soon as I opened the door, this gigantic snake was crawling down the screen door on the outside. Immediately, I screamed and called for Terry. I cried and told him it was a massive snake on the screen door.

He came running with a small shoe because he thought I was exaggerating. When he saw the snake on the door, he jumped, ran, and grabbed his gun. He ran out the back door to the front door and started shooting at the snake. However, he did not hit the snake with one bullet. He made the snake mad, so the snake hissed and jumped off the porch at him. By then, everyone was looking at the door and came running and trying to help. My brother, Marvin, is a mechanic and has always worked on cars, so one guy named Michael Davis was there getting his car fixed. He ran up to grab some bed rails because we were changing our full-sized bed to a queen-size one. So, he held the bed rails and hit the snake on the head. My brother Kelly ran out there to help kill the snake as well. By that time, I was terrified and crying. But, when Michael held the snake up, I saw how long it was, and he screamed at me and said it was a water moccasin. I had always heard the saying that snakes come when a woman is pregnant because they can smell the milk. Is that true? However, this snake scared me to death. I cried the entire day and could not stop thinking about that snake. In my seventh month, my back hurt even worse after this incident.

Later that night, when I tried to lie down, all I could see were snakes everywhere. I did not even make it to my mother's house to eat breakfast or anything else. However, my back continued to get worse. So, I asked my mom if I could come and stay with her. Of course, she said yes, and I did. Then Terry came later, and she told me that my back should not be hurting this bad and that I needed to go to the doctor. I told her it was on a Sunday and that I had an appointment to see my doctor on Monday because it was time for my weekly checkup. The next day, I was at my doctor's appointment, and my blood pressure was high. He told me my birth pressure was 280 over 130, which was not good. He also told me I was keeping fluids and that my body could set up for toxemia, which the medical term is Preeclampsia.

Preeclampsia, formerly called toxemia, is when pregnant women have high blood pressure, protein in their urine, and swelling in their legs, feet, and hands. https://www.webmd.com/ baby/preeclampsia-eclampsia#1
So, I immediately went to the emergency room in Starkville because he feared I would harm the baby if I developed too much toxemia.

Four
HOPE FOR PAIN

Hungry, Starving, Can't Eat. Got to go Somewhere.

Dr. Locke told me I had to go to the emergency room immediately and that my mother had to drive me there. This part was so funny because my mother couldn't move. She looked at me and quietly asked, "Can you drive?" I told her, "Yes, I can." She smiled, and then we looked back at the doctor and waited for further instructions. We were both hungry because I had promised her a big breakfast at the Waffle House.
Waffle House is a famous small restaurant known for waffles as their signature breakfast food.

  I told Mama that as soon as the doctor's visit was over, we would get something to eat, and everything would be fine once we left the hospital. However, that plan did not happen; that was just the beginning. I went straight to the emergency room, the third floor, and the pregnancy ward. When I got there, I had to undress and get hooked up to many machines and monitors, including the ones that monitor my baby's heartbeat. Because my blood pressure was so high, I had to always lie on my side. My mother was right by my side, and she got my cellular phone and called Terry off work and my sisters.

By the time she got off, Dr. Locke had explained that the University Medical Center in Jackson specializes in neonatal care and that an ambulance would transport me there. He told my mother that if my blood pressure continued to be high, the doctors there would probably do a C-section or induce Labor to have the baby.

Cesarean delivery (C-section) is a surgical procedure to deliver a baby through incisions in the abdomen or uterus. www.mayoclinic.org

Induce Labor-. Labor induction is the stimulation of uterus contractions during pregnancy, before Labor begins on its own, to achieve a vaginal birth. www.mayoclinic.org

He told us that the hospital in Jackson is the one that was a well-known hospital for delivering premature births and that they would take good care of me. He told Mom to tell Terry to bring clothes for a few days because we would be there awhile. By then, Terry came through the door looking worried and constantly asking me how I felt. I assured him I was okay. I felt good and did not have a headache or anything, but I was so hungry. The nurse checked my vitals and blood pressure, which was still in the 200s.

She told me that the ambulance was ready to transport me to Jackson. I told Mom to go home because they would probably monitor me when I arrived, but nothing more. She agreed, and by the time Renee got there, she looked worried and said they would come on later.

Emergency medical technicians (EMTs) and paramedics respond to emergency calls, performing medical services and transporting patients to medical facilities (https:// www.bls.gov/ooh/healthcare/emts-and-paramedics.htm).

The road trip to Jackson was a bumpy one and filled with EMTs. Jackson, Mississippi, was two hours away, and Terry trailed the ambulance. The EMT asked if I had a headache or any pain. I told him no, and that I was okay but hungry. He told me I should get a tray if the doctors approved it when we arrived in Jackson because it was almost dinnertime.

***University Medical Center, Jackson, Mississippi.** Finally, we are here! That was the bumpiest ride ever! I am surprised that the ride did not put me into Labor! I was so glad that the ride was over. They took me to the third floor, Labor, and Delivery, and assigned me a room. The doctor came in and told me the plans for delivering my baby. He told me that according to my charts, my baby weighs almost three pounds. Because of the low birth weight, I needed two steroid shots, one each day, to finish the development of the baby's lungs.

Steroid shots-antenatal steroid treatments usually consist of two injections, 24 hours apart. We use between 25 and 33 weeks to speed up the development of the baby's lungs. https:// www.ncbi.nlm.nih.gov/

The doctor also told me they would give me some medicine to help decrease my blood pressure. He ordered the first shot of steroids and called the cafeteria for a specific food tray, free of sodium and pork products. The first shot was not bad at all. It was given in the buttocks. The doctor told me to rest as much as possible and not worry or stress because it could add to more complications.

The next day, at the same time, I was given my second steroid shot. The doctor returned for another visit and told me that tomorrow, at 5:00 P.M., he would induce my Labor because the baby was in the correct position. He told me that it would be a vaginal delivery. He stated that my blood pressure was steady at 155 over 40. The medicine worked for the last 24 hours, but my swelling worsened.

He told me he recommended an epidural and spinal tap so my blood pressure would not increase during the Labor and delivery.

Epidural is regional anesthesia that blocks pain in a particular body region to relieve pain. https:// www.asahq.org/

Spinal A spinal block is spinal anesthesia often called
"spinal" lidocaine that is injected below the spinal column directly into the spinal fluid, which provides pain relief for as long as 2 hours. https:// americanpregnancy.org/

Later that day, the doctor came in and stated that around 3:00 P.M. on the 18th of June, the anesthesiologist would take me to another room to do the epidural and spinal tap. Then, later he would come back to put a cervix ripening in to start the labor process. He said that the cervix ripening would be in the walls of the cervix, stay about an hour, and once removed, I should be close to delivery. The doctor said that once the cervix ripens, it should dilate to eight to nine centimeters after that, which means to be ready to push and deliver my baby into the world.

Cervical ripening is a normal process of softening and opening the cervix before labor starts. The cervix is stiff and closed throughout the pregnancy to hold your baby inside your uterus. But during Labor, cervical dilation (widening) allows your baby to pass through your birth canal

(https://my.clevelandclinic.org/health/ treatments/ 22165-cervical- opening#:~:text=What%20is%20cervical% 20ripening%3F,pass%20through%20your%2 0birth%20can al

Ripen your cervix-Sometimes synthetic prostaglandins, typically placed inside the vagina, are used to thin or soften (ripen) the cervix. A small tube (catheter)
with an inflatable balloon on the end inserted into the cervix. **Filling the balloon with saline and resting it against the inside of the cervix helps ripen the cervix. https://www.mayoclinic.org**

After the doctor left my room, all my family was there: my mother, all my sisters but one- (Jeanette, Renee, Joyce, but Willyne lived in Florida), my brothers but one (Kelly, Marvin, Lil. Jr. Corey, and Gary-Timothy lives in Minnesota), Terry's mother, and sister-Linda. I tried to put on a smiling face, but I was exhausted. I was so tired that I didn't even remember them leaving. Terry said I had fallen asleep. But my mother did not go; she stayed. I was so happy she stayed.

Five
HOPE AND DELIVERY
The 18th of June 1999! The 19th of June 1999! Ready to Deliver. Tired. Come on! Let's Get This Over With.

Early on the 18th, Dr. Graves came in to start the process of delivery of our small, beautiful child. I was finally right-minded enough to catch his name. I looked at his name tag, something I had not done for the last two days I had been there. Dr. Graves told me that the anesthesiologist would be in to do the epidural and spinal. After that, he would ripen the cervix to start my contractions and Labor. Before Dr. Graves left, the anesthesiologist was there with a wheelchair to whisk me away for these procedures. My mother and Terry asked if they could go with us. They said yes but had to wait in a small waiting room, which they didn't mind. While in the room, I had to sit on the side of the bed with my gown pulled down in the front, and two of the anesthesiologists went to work. They told me to be as still as possible, which I did. They started with the epidural, which seemed like they were putting a line of medicine in my backbone. I do not know if there were needles are not, but I felt so good. I felt my body flush. It was like a release from the last few days of pain and hurt. It felt like a sense of being free-if that makes sense. This procedure took about 30 minutes or an hour, I cannot remember. Next came the spinal injection, which I started to feel free and so good when the medicine kicked in. I felt like myself, which I have not felt in the last few weeks. Once the procedure was over. Terry and Mother looked at me with worried faces. They both said that I looked strange and had some redness on my face. I told them I felt good and had no pain, which scared them. My mother just stood in the background with a concerned look. Later, I asked her about it. She says she was praying, and God told her I would be all right. The doctors came in with the nurse when we returned to the room. He explained the ripening of the cervix procedures and asked us whether we had any questions. Since we had no questions, he told us he would start immediately. He asked if I wanted my mother to stay because Terry automatically stayed there. I told him I did not care, but it was up to her. She said that she would stay. And with that, Dr. Graves started the procedure. He raised the bed as high as it could go and then lowered the head of the bed as low as it could go, with the bottom part still elevated. Then, the doctor placed my legs into stirrups on the bed's end. He inserted some gel, and then the cervix ripened. It felt so uncomfortable, and my stomach started to cramp. He told me he would check it in about 10 minutes. He lowered me back to a stable position on the bed and said we must wait and let the cervix ripened do its job.

My stomach started to get sharp pains and constant cramps, which were the start of contractions, but I must have dozed off because about 10 minutes, the nurse came in and said it was time to take the cervix ripening out. Terry asked her, "That's quick?" She told him, "Yes because the doctor said 10 minutes." Terry told her he thought the doctor said he would be back to check on it in 10 minutes, but she assured Terry that she was doing what he told her to do. Once again, I returned to an uncomfortable position. She took the tongs and pulled the ripened out. She positioned my bed back into a comfortable place. Then she left. About an hour later, the doctor returned to check the cervix and said the ripened should have me at about five centimeters. And if so, he would take it out. If not, he will leave it in for about 20 more minutes. Terry told Dr. Graves that the nurse had returned about 10 minutes after he had just put the ripening in and taken it out. He looked at Terry strangely and asked, "Who told her to do that?" Terry told him, "She said you told her to take it out. I told her you said you would check it in about 10 minutes, but she's told me she was doing her job." Dr. Graves paged her to my room and asked her why she took it out. She told him she thought that was what he told her to do. She says he told her to return in 10 minutes to take it out. He was furious and fussed at her right on the spot. The nurse started crying and said she was sorry. He told her I bet you are sorry because now this lady is only one centimeter, and I cannot put it back in. The doctor told her not only did he put the baby in danger but me as well. He said that her blood pressure might go back up, and the epidural might wear off, which would cause more stress. He told her that now we wait and hope for the best. He told her to meet him in his office. He turned to me and apologized, saying we must wait, and that is all we can do. We must wait for nature to do its job and for me to get the other nine centimeters.

Nine centimeters! Contraction!

Contractions are hitting harder and returning about five minutes apart. Next door, it was a young lady screaming, "Take it out! This thing is hurting me. It hurts! Oh my God!" She screamed again as I heard the doctors say, "Push, and you have to calm down!" The doctor told her, "Stop tensing up and give me the hardest push you got for me." Immediately I panicked. I got frightened and looked at my mother. By then, my brothers and sisters walked in Marvin, Gary, Kelly, Lil Jr., Renee, Joyce, and Jeanette. My sister Willyne stayed in Florida but constantly called and asked Renee how I was. I cannot remember who was there. I was in so much pain. All I know is that those contractions were coming harder. My back throbbed and hurt so badly that I told them to call the doctor. But before the words came out, the doctor walked through the door but with a different nurse. The doctor shook all my family members' hands and told them he needed to check my cervix to see how many centimeters I had dilated. He asked me if I wanted them all to stay here. I told him yes, and I didn't care what they did. I was ready to get this over, but then my mind reflected on the lady next door. She was screaming, but I knew I would not act like that. I knew that to get this pain and deliver this baby; I had to do what the doctors told me to do. I needed to call on the name of God. I prayed, but my prayer stopped when my brother Marvin said, "I am going to step out. Don't anybody want to see him check on her?" They all left, even Terry tried to leave, but the doctor told him not you, husband stay. Terry looked like a scared little boy that needed to be saved by someone, and I then heard his mother, Bo, and his sister Linda's voices out there. So, it seemed like Terry felt better and returned to hold my hand. Dr. Graves checked my cervix and said I was ready to start the delivery process. He told us he would scrub and prepare the staff for my baby boy's delivery. The doctor left and told my family we were preparing to deliver this baby. He told them they could return to see me and then wait in the nursery's waiting room. They came back in and kissed me and left out. It was delivery time, and the doctor returned, raised the bed higher, placed my feet in stirrups, and told me that my blood pressure was still stable. I was confused because I thought there was another room for delivery; however, if you know what I meant, the feeling left quickly. Now, the doctor told me to push. Oh my God. I was in pain, and as Terry held my hand, I squeezed it and continued to push.

I started to push when the doctor told me to. He stated that I was crowning and that he could see the baby's head coming. He told me to "push" hard again, which I did, and I heard a cry. It was my baby boy. I felt so much relief, and the pain was gone. The doctor held the baby up and told us we had a beautiful baby girl. Terry and I looked at each other and said in unison, "A girl?" The doctor in Starkville told us that we were having a boy. However, we were so happy, but she was so tiny. I could not even hold her because she was so small. My miracle girl had arrived, and I thank God.

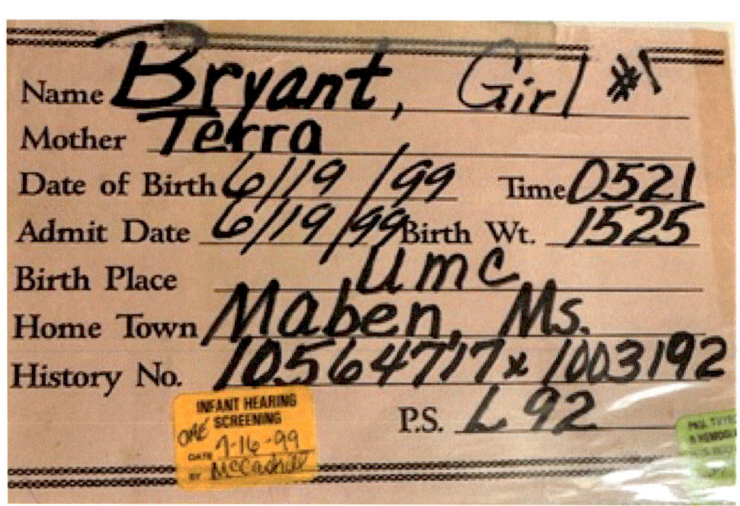

Chapter Six
HOPE -GROWTH-AND BIRTH WEIGHT

Beautiful! Tiny! No teeny! Pale skin! Observance! Lovable!

My baby. My sweet girl. Soon after delivery. I did not get to hold her because she was so small. The doctor held her up and showed her to me. She looked like a little weenie dog, so tiny but sweet. I looked at her and said, "God, let my baby be all right." I blew a kiss at her. I was so exhausted. The nurse told me she would be in a Neonatal Intensive Care Unit (NICU).

The Neonatal Intensive Care Unit is an Intensive Care Unit specializing in the care of ill or premature newborn infants,
www.wikipedia.com

The nurse told me that she would be in the NICU and would check all her vital signs and do the tests they do for our babies. The other nurses cleaned me and the area up, and I looked at Terry. He was crying and laughing at the same time. After about 30 minutes, the room was clean. New linens were put on the bed, a sponge bath, and a new gown. I was ready to see my family; my blood pressure had started evaluating but was stable, which meant I could see all my family members simultaneously. They all came in and told me what they saw when they took my daughter to the NICU and that she was so tiny but had her eyes open. My brother Marvin said, "She's a fighter. She will be an all-right Baby" (Baby is the nickname my family gave me). I shook my head but was worn out and tired, but I tried not to show my feelings. The nurse came back and told me that my baby girl weighed three pounds six ounces and that she would be in the hospital until she gained up to five pounds. I asked if I could breastfeed her because I heard that it helps her to develop faster. She told me the doctor would not allow it because I would be released soon, meaning I had to leave my baby in Jackson alone. I started to cry, and I suddenly asked God to keep my blood pressure high enough that I would be able to stay with her. The nurse reassured me that my baby would be fine and that I could go home and finish the nursery if I had not already done so.

I thought about the nursery and knew our little work had to be changed because the doctor told us we were having a boy instead of a girl. I can make the baby's nursery more girlish and move things around. The nurse checked my vitals and told me I could visit the NICU in a few minutes and see my baby girl. Immediately my tiredness left, and I could not wait to see her. (It was amazing how my strength returned and that all that pushing and aching did not matter anymore.)

Those 20 minutes seem like an eternity. I was able to see my daughter. The nurse brought me a wheelchair. But I told her that I wanted it to walk.

When Terry and I arrived at the NICU, we had to scrub up from our arms to our elbows and put on a hairnet, mask, and blue gown. The nurse at the station told us that the scrubbing helped prevent the spread of germs. She escorted us up to the incubator that my daughter was in.

The incubator and enclosed apparatus provide an enclosed environment for protecting premature or unusually small babies. www.dictionary.com

I saw so many babies there. Some babies were small and underweight, and some babies were at an average birth rate but had monitors on them. My daughter was in the center of the room. The babies were all placed in the Oval-shaped setting around the NICU room. I looked at my baby's name tag. It said, Bryant baby girl, June 1999-Three pounds six ounces. Then my eyes settled on my baby. She had so many wires and machines, and she lay on her back. I watched her chest rise and fall, and I tapped lightly on the incubator. I said to her, "I see you, baby girl. It's me and your daddy. Can you hear me? I love you so much. I wish I could hold you to tell you how much I love you." I guess she knew my voice because she started stretching and moving. She blinked her eyes she looked just like my brother, Little Junior-Big head and "tight" eyes (lol-laughing out loud).

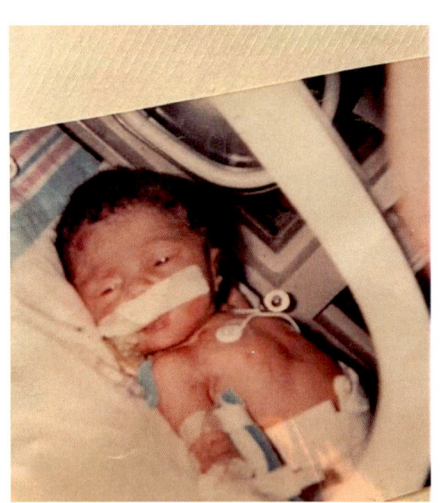

My baby was so precious. Terry and I were crying softly as we only had 10 minutes to visit. While standing there, the nurse came over and opened one of the compartments so that we could touch her. We played with her hand and just touched and rubbed on her. Then, time was up. It seemed like only two minutes, but the same nurse returned and explained how they would feed my baby. She told me that since she is so tiny, they would start her feeding with a regular-sized shot needle type with a little pointer that they will slowly release milk into her mouth. She said they would begin her with ten ccs of milk and work their way up.

cc's stands for the cubic centimeter-A measure of volume in the metric system

She said that since she was so tiny, her stomach must expand, and after the milk is kept down in her stomach and not throwing it back up; they would increase the doses to three ccs each time until she reached the bottle. I understood this but hated that I could not feed her. After her explanation, we said, "See you later," and walked back to my room. We talked a little with my family, told them what the nurse told us, and asked them to pray for my baby girl.

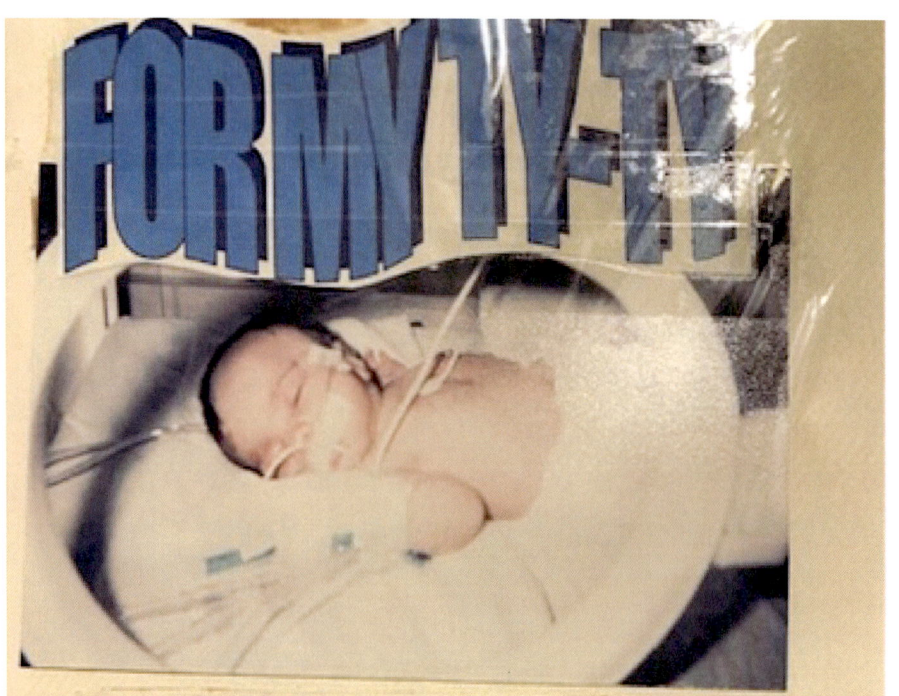

FOR MY TY-TY

Just checking on my little princess.

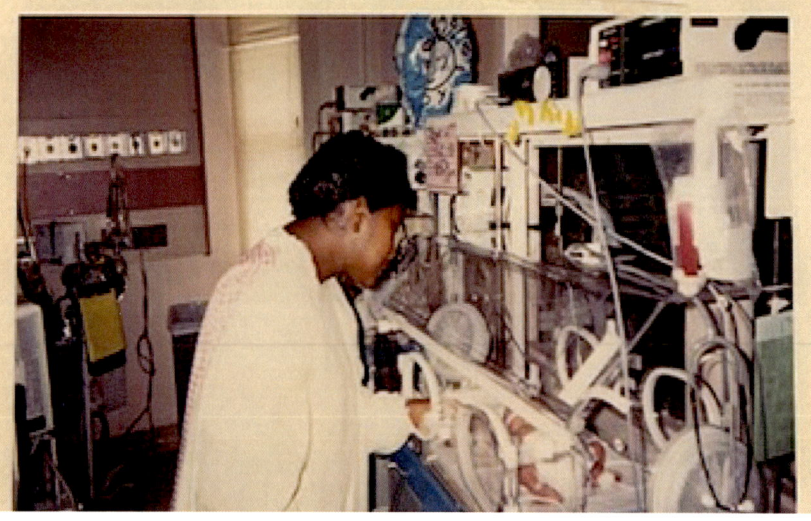

Seven
HOPE AND NEONATAL CARE

Third day! Don't Want to Leave! Bless my Baby! Still so Tiny!

It was the 22nd of June 1999. My blood pressure was back to normal. The doctor told me that if it stayed that way all day, I would be discharged and sent home tomorrow.

Discharge-tell someone that they can or must leave a place or situation. www.dictionary.com

Before the "being released" news, I was happy we were there with our daughter. We have visited the Neonatal Intensive Care Unit every visiting hour, which ranged from 6 A.M., 9 A.M., 12 P.M., 4 P.M., and the last visit at 6:00 P.M., The doctor, came in and told me that I would be discharged and free to go home. I got so depressed and prayed to God that he would let my blood pressure back up so I could stay. Dr. Graves sprung this news on me around 8:30 A.M. that morning, and I felt so bad. I did not want to leave my baby in Jackson and travel home to Starkville, two and a half hours away. I looked at Terry; he already knew what I was thinking and assured me everything would be all right.

It was now 9:00 A.M., and it was time to see our beautiful little girl. We scrubbed up, put on a mask and a gown, and went inside to see our little girl. She was sleeping and so tiny. I prayed and tapped on the incubator, and she immediately started moving and opening her eyes. I must have said this aloud, "I wish I could hold you, little girl. And I love you so much." The nurse asked us if we had held her since she's been in NICU. I told her no. She asked did I wanted to keep her, and I immediately said yes. She opened an incubator and unhooked some of the cords because there were many of them. She unhooked the cables from her ankle, took her out, and handed me my beautiful little girl. She was so tiny but very alert, and it seemed like she was staring at me, saying, "Mommy, where have you been? Is this you? You are so beautiful." Laughing out loud. Then, I let Terry hold her. He was crying—big crybaby. Please don't make me start crying. I was doing fine. We just looked at her and smiled. I thought, Terra, you created a beautiful little girl, and she will grow and be unique.

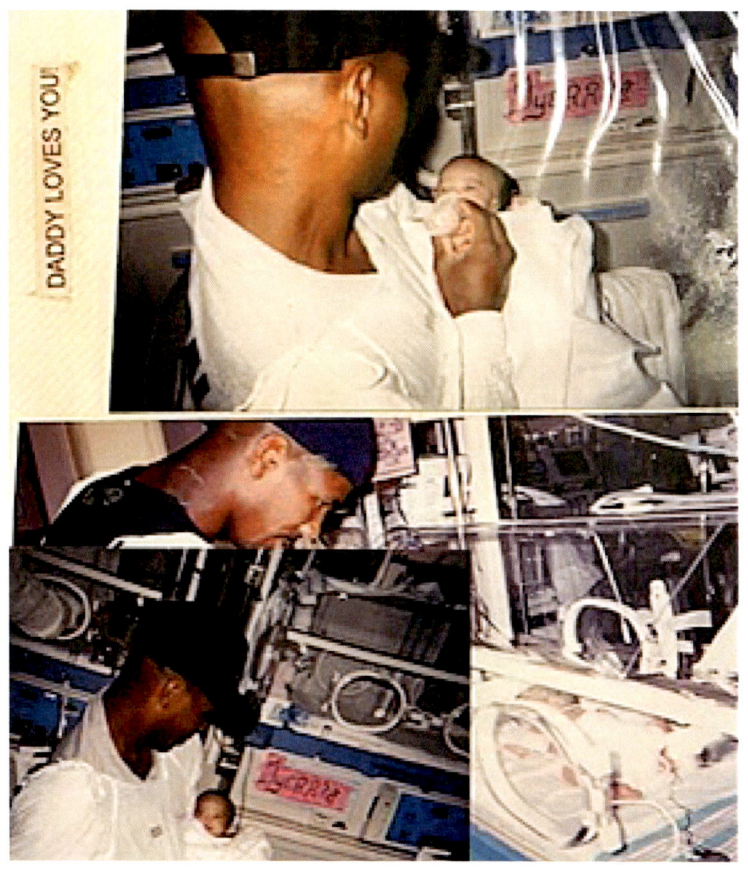

After about five minutes, the nurse asked, "Do we want to feed her? We both said yes simultaneously, but I told Terry he could feed her first. After he finished, I held her again. We took lots of pictures, and then it was time to go. Terry said, "See you later, little girl." We took off all our stuff and returned to the room. When we got back, the lady was there for us to name the baby. My sister Joyce had already given us a name, one combined with both. Terra and Terry, which was Tyerria. She also gave me a middle name and told Joyce I would name her that, but I wanted to call her V'Zon because she was my Vision, which God had granted. He saw my Vision of wanting a baby that would never happen. So, my dream became a reality and God blessed my Vision. I thought about Joyce and how she would poke her lips out and say, "I told you a poor (skinny) self to name her something else, but I liked it."

When I told Joyce this, she laughed and said I did good, but nobody wanted to be called Vision. She didn't know my spelling of it. I told the lady (the name lady) that my daughter's name would be Tyerria Tanv'zon Bryant. The "Tan" in front of the "V'Zon" was a part of my middle name, Tannette. I knew I had to put the Vision in there as a constant reminder of my Vision for a family and for a daughter that took me so long to conceive. I thank the name lady and silently thank God for such a blessing.

Eight
HOPE IN CHRIST

Released! Discharge! Not Wanting to Leave! Crying! I Can't Leave my Baby.

On the third day, the 23rd of June, the nurse came in to check my vital signs around breakfast. She said that Dr. Graves would come and make his rounds today. She told me my blood pressure had returned to normal, 120 over 80. She told me that she thought I would be discharged from the hospital today. I looked at her funny and said, "I don't want to leave my baby." She told me that my baby girl was doing fine, and as soon as she gained five pounds, she will be released as well.

Release-the act of setting free or letting go. www.merrianwebster.com

  She asked if we had gotten her nursery done. I told her no. She told us that when we get home, we can get our baby's nursery done how we want it to be. Shortly afterward, Dr. Graves came in and told us our big news. I was getting released, but Tyerria would have to stay in the hospital for about two months. He informed us that she was healthy and still taking those two ccs of milk and not throwing it up. Dr. Grave told us she has a little stomach that must expand slowly. I immediately started crying and told him I did not want to leave my baby. He assured me that she was in good hands, and deep inside, I knew she was with the best doctors in the world.

Terry and I thanked him. He told me all the paperwork should take about an hour and then left the room. I tried to calm down, and when it seemed like I was about to lose it, my two cousins, Sean and Stan, walked into the room. Terry greeted them and told them that I would be released today.

Sean and Stan are my first cousins on my mother's side, Uncle Bay and Aunt Lena Mae's children. Uncle Bay is the brother of my mother, Cora. Before this time, my cousins and I would only talk at family reunions, funerals, or when we visited each other during the summer or something like that. But since my time in Jackson, we had become very close, and they checked on me frequently, and our relationship remains close. We chatted briefly but were interrupted when the nurse came in with the discharge paper. She asked Terry where he parked and told him to go and get the car. She told him to bring the vehicle to the front, and she would finish helping me gather my things. Sean and Stan told us we were welcome to stay with them anytime. I told them we might take them up on their offer, which we did. While talking, Terry returned, and Sean asked him where he had parked the car. He told him right in front of the hospital and left the car running but got the keys with him. Stan told him that he better go and get his car because Jackson is known for stealing cars, and they would break in his window and get the car in a matter of minutes. Boy, Terry flew out of there!

Minutes later, the nurse brought the wheelchair, and my two cousins walked us down to the front lobby. My heart was breaking because I didn't want to leave my baby. I wanted to see her again, but it was not close to visiting hours yet. We had a couple more hours before that time. The elevator ride seemed like forever, but we finally were out of the elevator to the hospital's front door. I hugged my cousins and told them that I would see them soon. Terry shook hands, and with that, we got in the car and left. I cried and cried and didn't want to leave. Terry was quiet but broke his silence when he asked if I wanted anything to eat. I wasn't hungry, and it seemed he wasn't either, so we headed down Highway 55 north out of Jackson to Starkville. After about two hours, we made it home. Our entire family was there. We were crying and hugging and laughing all at once. My family assured me everything would be fine, and they would help with the baby's room. I started feeling better and said I would love for them to do just that. Later that day, I called every hour until nine o'clock P.M. to check on Tyerria. I gave my family the number, and they called as many times as they wanted to check on Tyerria. We were happy that they gave us an update every time. After my family left, I got ready for bed but could not sleep. My stomach turned into knots, and I cried in Terry's arms.

Finally, I went to sleep. The next day, I woke up with my baby in my mind. I entered my baby's room and started putting the ABC pictures on the wall. I bought a white crib and a bassinet. Her bed consisted of Mickey Mouse and Minnie Mouse bedding, with a Disney character mobile. My sister Renee and two nieces, Ratty (Talekia) and Shayne, helped decorate her room, and we put foam connecting blocks on the floor with ABCs printed on them. Renee put up the blinds and curtains, and the entire nursery consisted of Mickey AND Minnie Mouse and some Looney Tune Characters. Ratty and Shayne hung up the clothes I had gotten from the two baby showers at Sudduth Elementary School, where I was a teaching assistant. The other shower came from my family. Also, they displayed teddy bears, other toys, and stuffed animals in her crib from the baby shower.

Working at the baby nursery, I found some peace at home. We were excited about bringing my little girl home. I knew she would only lie in her nursery briefly because she would end up in bed with us. Once we found a good stopping point, my family left. I showered, lay on the couch, called, and checked on Tyerria. After getting a good report, I went to sleep. It was the third day at home (two and a half days) without my baby. The next day, I woke up around nine o'clock AM. I called and checked on Tyerria, and the nurse told me she was up to three ccs of milk. I was so happy and said my baby was easing up to drinking a whole bottle. Thank you, God! So afterward, my sister Joyce called me and said she was having a birthday party for her grandson Taytay. She told us to come and that it would start around four o'clock PM. I told her we would be, but the day seemed to drag along, so I just sat in my room until it was time. Constantly, I prayed that my baby would gain those five pounds soon and come home. Around four o'clock PM, we went around Joyce's house to her grandson's birthday party. All the family was over there. We went into her house, laughing and talking. Each one of us had different conversations at the same time but knew what we were saying. I mostly gave them an update about Tyerria and sat on the couch. During the party, my sister Jeanette called Joyce's house phone. Joyce answered and told all of us to be quiet. We all stopped talking, and for some strange reason, my heart started to beat hard, and my stomach had butterflies. When Joyce hung up the phone, she said, "Terra and Terry, you all need to call Jackson because the doctor said they have been trying to contact you. Something wrong with the baby." I got up, got my cell phone, went outside, and called the NICU in Jackson. The nurse told me the doctors wanted to talk to us about Baby Bryant and put me on hold. **Oh my God! My heart stopped! And I was frozen and could not move!** Finally, Dr. Grave got on the phone. He said, "Mrs. Bryant, Is your husband

there with you?" I answered, "Yes." He told me, "Good. I need you all to come to Jackson right away. Your baby stopped breathing and was placed on a breathing machine ventilator. She was blue in the face." My heart stopped beating, and I was terrified. Then he said, "Thank God she started back breathing, but she was on life support," Dr. Graves continued. He stated that while briefing the oncoming staff around seven o'clock PM and giving them an update about each baby, something told him to turn around and return to the NICU for another walkthrough. Dr. Graves ignored that feeling at first, but the feeling grew stronger. So, he told the staff to walk with him while he checked on the babies again. That is when he saw that Tyerria had turned blue in the face.
He told us that he immediately started giving orders to get the infant CPR bag, and they went to work, giving her CPR.

CPR-cardiopulmonary risk reduction is an emergency life-saving procedure performed when the heart stops beating.
www.cpr.heart.org

Dr. Graves said, "Currently, she is on life support to help her with breathing. We need you or your husband to come, so we can run some tests to see what caused her to stop breathing." I told him it would take us about two hours to arrive, but we were on the way. At about that time, my family, Terry, and I were crying and in shock. Dr. Graves told us to be careful and that he was going home to shower but had instructed the nurse to call him as soon as we arrived. Then, he would meet us at UMC hospital." I told him, " Okay, " Thank you, and then hung up.

I told my family what the doctor told me, and they started praying and hugging us. Joyce told us to be careful and that she would pray for us. We left and went back home to get some clothes. My sister Jeanette told her children's father, Louis, who is a Pastor, what happened. He met us at the front door of our house when we were coming out to leave. Jeanette and Louis made their way up the steps and asked us if he could pray for us. We told him yes. He told us to join hands and began praying. I can't remember all the exact words Louis prayed for, but I remember some and how hard he prayed for us. He asked God for healing and said this baby was our miracle baby. He reminded God about how long it took them to conceive this baby; How I went into Labor early, and how this baby had already survived those things. He asked God to let His Will be Done and let our baby live so we can give her back to him. He reminded God about Hannah when she gave Samuel back to Him.

1st Book of Samuel: Hannah Dedicates Samuel to the Lord. 1st Samuel 1:10-17, 20.

Louis told God that he knew us when we were little children, that we had always been good people, and that we were still his family. He asked for God's blessing as we travel and requested this in the mighty name of Jesus Christ, Amen.

See, Louis was my brother-in-law for years. He has three children with my sister Jeanette-Tessia, Talekia, and Danta. Although they both are married to someone else-He knows us, still, to this day, we are his family, and he is ours. Terry and I hugged him tightly, with tears running down our faces. We hugged everyone and headed to Jackson, MS. It was around six o'clock that evening.

On the way to Jackson, my cousin Dee that lives in Jackson, Mississippi, called me and said that Linda (our cousin) got a call from my mother and told them what had happened. She told us that we were welcome to stay with her if we wanted to. We told her the doctor's exact words and said we would love to stay with her. I told her we would call her after we made it to the hospital, chatted a little more, and then we ended the call. To Jackson, I prayed and reminded God of the gift He has given us. I reminded him of His greatness and the blessing of answering prayers of conceiving a child.

Nine
HOPE IN HYDRO AND HOSPITAL

**I can't breathe. I just wanted to see her.
Please, God, bless my child.**

Terry parked the car, and we arrived in less than two hours. Yes, he was pushing the gas on the pedal, and I prayed we would not get pulled over. God answered that prayer and many others. We got out, power-walked through the ICU, and then to the third floor of the NICU. We checked in, and the nurse told us to wait as she called Dr. Graves. She hung up and said that he would be there in less than 30 minutes and that we were allowed to see Tyerria. We scrubbed our hands, arms, and elbows to the elbow, which was standard procedure. We were so quiet and didn't know what to say to each other or the nurse. We put on our masks and gowns, which was a routine. We walked around slowly around the corner to her incubator. As I walked, I prayed, not just for the Tyerria but for all those precious babies. When we went around the corner, Tyerria was hooked up with many tubes and a breathing mask over her face. The nurse told us what every machine was, but the one that I stopped at was the life support machine. **OH MY GOD! MY BABY!** The nurse assured us that the machine was turned down from 100% to 30%, from where it started earlier that day. She told us that she is a fighter and is breathing more independently but will not come off until Dr. Grave runs more tests to see why she went from being healthy to becoming sick suddenly. She opened the door and told us we could touch her as much as we wanted. By then, I was crying, praying, and at a loss for words. I was so worried about my child, and I wished I could do something to remove the pain. I know I shouldn't have been nervous and always trusted in God. But as a new mother, it was hard. I only wanted to shield, protect, and remove her pain, but I could not. Terry and I had been lost in our thoughts until we did not even see Dr. Graves come in. He had a serious but caring look on his face. Dr. Graves told us to follow him to the conference room. We removed our gowns, hats, and masks and threw them in the bin. Then, we followed behind him. Dr. Graves told us to sit in the conference room, then explained what he thought had happened to Tyerria. He told us that Baby Bryant had been doing good. She passed all the infant checkups and has taken the ccs of milk. He said he did not know what happened and had pondered over this mystery himself. He asked us many questions, such as if we had had any family illness that could be an underlying factor in why she got sick. He wondered whether we had anyone in our families with heart disease, a hole in the heart, or cancer. He asked us to think about any childhood illnesses or any history of allergies. He asked us to think hard about all family members, siblings, their children, or even if we have been sick. He asked us to think about our grandparents, aunts, and uncles who had experience dealing with any sicknesses as a child. After that, he asked if we knew any family members that ever dealt with anything like this or if their children had any experiences like Tyerria being fine one day and then stopping breathing the next. Next, he told us they were preparing to run many tests and blood work.

Although she is tiny, Dr. Graves stated that she was given sedatives to be put to sleep, and an MRI would be performed to provide stronger results. The MRI will look deeply into the organs and the tissues. MRI.

Magnetic Resonance Imaging scan produces detailed images of the organs and tissues in the body. www.MedicaNewstoday.com

After the MRI, he stated that she would have a CT SCAN done to look at the bones and get another different angle of the heart, lungs, and other organs.

CT SCAN-A computed tomography (CT or CAT) scan allows doctors to see inside your body. It uses a combination of X-rays and a computer to create pictures of your organs, bones, and other tissues. It shows more detail than a regular X-ray. Webmd.com.

Dr. Graves told us that the nurses and technicians would take her down in a few minutes if we permitted him to run all these tests. We nodded yes in unison and told him we would do whatever it took to discover why our baby was sick. Dr. Graves stood up and said that we could wait in the NICU waiting room and that the nurse would come and get us as soon as he had some answers. We all stood up, thanked him, headed to the NICU, and went to the waiting room. However, it was getting late, and the nurse told us they were still running tests. She told us to go and get a good night's sleep and that we could see Tyerria once all the tests were done. It took about two days to find out what Tyerria was facing. Dr. Grave gave us some speculations of what he thought may be the problem. He felt she had a hole in her heart or lungs, or the lungs may not fully develop. He told us he thought maybe it was a brain problem, a tumor, or a rare disease. He said Tyerria had undergone several MRIs, CAT scans, and other tests I can't pronounce. Dr. Grave told us he had one more test, which is common in premature babies. This test calls for a more in-depth look at the brain using blue dye. He assured us she was still hanging on and had no significant change, which he said was good. It was good that she had not taken a turn for the worse, and it was bad because they were given regular antibiotics that were not working. Also, he told us that Tyerria had lost six ounces, which was underweight. So now she's back to three pounds.

Terry and I were in shock and continued calling on Jesus's name. Dr. Graves asked us for permission to do some procedures and said he hated having her undergo them because of all the radiation, but he knew it had to be done. We also agreed, and he left us to complete the procedures. Terry and I were quiet and prayed for a miracle for our miracle child that I didn't think I could not have and still could not hold in my arms. It seems that just when I was about to break down and cry, a stillness and a calmness came over me. I began to praise God and thank Him for the blessings He has given us. I praised Him for the answer that He was about to provide us with and the answer that my daughter would be healed. I was walking around, crying, and giving thanks. I bet Terry probably thought I was crazy, but I stopped crying and told him that God told me our baby would be all right. I told Terry that they would find out what was wrong with her. I told him that God was good and that we would bring our baby home soon. About an hour later, Dr. Graves returned and told us he had finally discovered what was medically wrong with Tyerria. He called it **Hydrocephalus**. He broke this down in laypeople's terms. Dr. Graves said they call it "**water head babies**." He saw how we looked and the look on our faces. But he told us quickly now that we know we can begin treatment. He gave the order to start the treatment before he came in. Then he sat down and explained to us what Hydrocephalus was and how Ty was infected by this disability.

Hydrocephalus comes from the Greek words: "Hydro," meaning water, and "cephalus," meaning head.

"Hydrocephalus is a chronic, neurological condition caused by an abnormal accumulation of cerebrospinal fluid (CSF) within cavities of the brain called ventricles, resulting in pressure on the brain. It affects over 1 million Americans, ranging from infants and older children to young and middle-aged adults, as well as seniors. There is currently no cure for hydrocephalus, but it can be treatable" https://www.hydroassoc.org/

He stated that she had meningitis, an infection that attacks the spinal fluids in the blood-brain and spinal cord. He asked me whether I had any illness during my first or second trimester of pregnancy. I told him I had the flu during my first trimester, a few weeks after getting pregnant. He said that is what caused this infection, meningitis. He told us that this could be corrected with antibiotics through an IV.

Intravenous (IV) refers to the administration of substances into the body through a vein or veins. IV therapy, therefore, works by delivering fluid directly into your veins www.infusionassociates.com

He told us that meningitis attacked the ventricles and caused them to close, so none of the Cerebral fluids could pass through. He told us that Tyerria's right ventricle was completely closed, which caused her to stop functioning on the right side. He told us that she had to undergo five weeks of intensive antibiotics, and hopefully, the right ventricle would open back up. He said they would shunt her head in the right ventricle if it didn't open back up. He hoped the antibiotics would correct this and open the right ventricle. He continued to provide us with some statistics and treatment plans. After that, Dr. Graves told us to go home or to a hotel and get some sleep. And we can see her tomorrow.

I felt like the weight of the world and my burdens were lifted, and I looked at Terry and told him that I knew God had her; God was going to protect and bless her. We hugged and praised God. We stood up, and on our way out, I called my cousin Dee and told her about Tyerria's diagnosis, and she insisted that we stay with her. We told her that we would get a hotel, but Dee told us to save that money, and we could sleep on her couch, or she would give us her bed. I told her the couch would be fine because it was almost 8 P.M., and I couldn't sleep. On the way to Dee's house, we stopped and got something to eat. It was almost nine o'clock PM. When we arrived, her daughter, Terra Renee, who has the same first name as mine, and my sister Renee. She told us to pull up in the driveway and she will park behind us, and we did. She says sometimes people fly by, and she didn't want our car to get hit. Plus, she had to go to work. We understood and made our way into the house; Dee came and greeted and hugged us and praised God for His blessing.

We sat on the couch and talked for some time; while talking, our other cousins made it into the house, Darrin, Pat-Poo, and Baby Sis (Sorry, I don't know their real names, only nicknames).

A nickname is a substitute for the proper name of a person a familiar place, person, or thing www.wikipedia.org

We talked to Darrin and some others for a while and bought some CDs and DVDs from Darrin. After Darrin left, we went to the shower, got comfortable on the couch, talked to Dee for a bit longer, then turned in for the night. Before we went to sleep, we told Dee we would leave early for the first visiting hour at 6:00 A.M. The next day, at about five o'clock that morning, we got up, thanked Dee for her hospitality, and for letting us stay with her while we checked on our daughter Tyerria. And she led us out of the house to leave. I was so thankful for my cousin Dee because we didn't know much about Jackson. We were exhausted but thankful because it was already late, and it would have been a waste of money to check in at a hotel. So, we were grateful that Dee told us to save that money and to come to stay with her (which we stayed several times). We went straight to the hospital and the second floor, the NICU, where Tyerria was still in. We knew the routine scrub, put on our masks and gloves, and went to see our baby girl. She was lying there helplessly hooked up to many machines and tubes in the mouth and through her nose. She had a wide forehead and looked like my brother Arthur (Lil Jr.) with short curly hair. She looked so peaceful, and my heart sank and melted simultaneously for my baby. After looking for a while, I tapped on the incubator window and called her name, "Hey Tyerria, Mommy's here. Hey, big girl. You are so strong, and I know you will come home soon. Hey, my precious baby girl." She must have heard my voice because she moved a little, turned her head, and blinked her eyes. She opened them for a few seconds, and Terry and I smiled.

Then, he tapped on the incubator and said, "Hey, Daddy, little girl. Daddy loves you; you get better, baby girl." He has started to tear up. We were teary-eyed, but we both had hopes and knew that God told us our baby girl would be coming home soon. He blessed our baby, our miracle girl. While we were visiting, the nurse came over and told us that the doctor had already given her the second round of antibiotics and that she would get stronger and stronger with every round. She told us that with each round, she started moving, and they would start back working on her weight. We thanked God and stayed for the entire visit.

When we headed to the front of the nursing station, she stopped us and told us that the 11 o'clock visiting hour was canceled due to most infants' next treatment. So, we headed to the cafeteria because we didn't want to leave the hospital. We walked in silence until we got there. My mind was racing, and I could imagine Terry was too. I thought about my baby girl. How powerful those antibiotics are, and I pray she would be receptive to them. "God! Please continue to help her. I'm desperate and in need of you. God, please bless my child," I said silently to myself. My imagination and thoughts continued until it was time to order our food. I can remember having pancakes, sausage, eggs, and a Coke. I was hungry, but my stomach was turning, so I knew to get a Coke to help ease my butterflies. Terry ordered the same thing, and we sat down and ate. Then, once finished, we got up and headed back outside to the car. We knew we had a few more hours to spend. So, we went to a few stores and browsed around. Then I told Terry to go to the North Side Mall in Clinton, Mississippi. On the way there, I saw Osh-Gosh-B-Gosh and Gap stores. I told Terry to stop, and once we got inside, I fell in love because it was full of baby clothes. I bought so much stuff for Tyerria that I had to give away new clothes because she never wore them. However, I had over $1,000 worth of stuff. And I only paid $200 or less for it. After I finished, we browsed around the mall but only bought a little. I went into Victoria's Secret, and Terry stayed outside and sat on the bench waiting for me.

While shopping, I got a call from the hospital. Instead of panicking, I felt peaceful and immediately answered the phone. The nurse called to let us know that the second treatment went well. They had already seen some improvements in her movements, and the nurse said that the next treatment would be before the evening hour. So, if we wanted to see her, we could come now and stay until after the 11 o'clock visit. It was probably around 10:30 A.M. I got off the phone, told Terry the excellent news, and returned to the hospital.

Ten
HOPELESS TURNS TO HOPEFUL

Alert! Looking Around! Smiling! Clear Eyes! My Sweetheart!

After several weeks of antibiotics, Tyerria is very alert and responds well, has her eyes opened, and is scanning her surroundings. While I look at her, I think about her journey from birth to now, five weeks later. The date is around the second week of July. She finally moved out of the incubator to a tabletop that did not have a glass covering. However, she still has a tube running inside her nose, an IV in her arm, and a small oxygen mask.

It was visiting hour, so Terry and I walked in and saw a semi-smiling bright-eyed little girl. She was just a joy to see. Her eyes and face were clear, and she was unattached from all those tubes, wires, and machines. She was out, **MIRACLE BABY!** While looking at her, my eyes filled with tears as I thanked God for His blessing and prayed that He would continue to bless and heal her. I prayed for her strength and ours as well. Terry was all smiles and just kept rubbing her face and arm. We were touching her and probably wishing the same, as we wanted to hug her. While in our thoughts, Dr. Graves told us that Tyerria was responding well and had about two more weeks of treatment left. He told us that if she continues to gain over five pounds and the infection does not return, she will come home soon. We were very optimistic about hearing that news.

Optimistic: feeling or showing hope for the future. www.merriam-Webster.com, 2021.

Every day, Tyerria continued to show strength and gained ounces. We went to visit her in July around the fourth, and we did the usual scrubbing of our hands and put on our gloves, caps, mask, and gowns. We were still glad and hopeful about how much our baby girl was improving, but when we turned the corner, Terry and I frowned in disbelief. Tyerria was tied down to the bed. Her hands were bound down! She had an IV in the vein of her forehead! We wondered what was going on. Tyerria looked like a prisoner in her small, opened incubator. We were heartbroken and could not understand what was happening, and then Terry got a little angry. He demanded to see the doctor and asked the nurse why Tyerria was strapped in her bed. I knew I could not understand what was happening. The nurse tried to reassure us that it was alright and that the doctor did this for a good reason, but Terry did not hear it. The nurse said that Dr. Graves was on the way and still tried to calm Terry down. As for me, I was breaking down inside and felt so bad for my little girl. Shortly afterward, Dr. Graves walked through the door. Terry took charge and told the doctor what he thought about Tyerria being strapped down on the table. Dr. Graves tried to speak, but Terry kept talking and demanding an answer. So, Dr. Graves stopped trying and told us to follow him back to her incubator. Terry was still fussing, so Dr. Graves had to raise his voice, but Terry still would not calm down. So, he told Terry to put his finger in her tiny hand. Terry looked at him like he was crazy at first but did it. Then, Terry asked him what the meaning behind this was. Dr. Graves told Terry to try and remove his finger from her grasp. Terry tried and tried, but he could not remove his hand. Terry told him he could not get his finger loose from her grip and did not want to hurt her. Dr. Graves said, "That's my point exactly. We had to scrap her down because she kept pulling her IV out, and when we tried to take it from her, she would not let go." He said they did not want to keep putting her IV back into her tiny arms and had to strap her down because she had a firm grip. He told us they had to strap her in the bed to keep the IV in place. Dr. Graves said, "She is a fighter and strong. She will hold that grip on you and not let it go until she is ready." Terry quickly found that out because she held onto his hand for the entire visiting hour. We were granted the chance to stay longer until she was tired of holding that grip on his hand. Terry and I were so embarrassed and continued to apologize to Dr. Graves and the nursing staff. They accepted our apologies and thought it was quite funny. We thanked them and were so glad that she was strong and showing strength.

WEEK FIVE: This was the last week of antibiotics, and Tyerria was more alert than ever. She was so observant and seemed to be taking everything in. She constantly turned her head from left to right, and this time, both grandparents were there for a visit (I told you earlier how Bo-Terry's mother said she wouldn't babysit or do this, but as you can see, she is right there). Tyerria was doing well, and I remembered saying a small prayer that these blessings would continue to overflow. We let the grandparents visit after us, and we were relieved and thankful that she was gaining weight. She was up to 4 lbs. and 15 oz. The nurse told us that she had a few more ounces and that we would take her home soon. We could not wait, and we felt overjoyed and blessed. The nurse told us that Dr. Parent, the neurologist, had ordered a shunt tapping to ensure all the infection was completely gone from her body.

Shunt tapping is the tapping of aspirating the shunt performed for both diagnostic reasons (e.g., evaluate for shunt infection and blockage) and therapeutic reasons...
www.emedicine.medspace.com, 2021.
   The nurse explained the procedure to us, which consisted of taking a needle and tube, filling it with

cerebrospinal fluid, and testing it to determine if any infection was still there. She told us that if there is not any infection, then there is a good chance Ty would be going home by the end of the week, which would be the 2nd week of August. She said that if there was any infection left, then there would be another week of antibiotics, and another spinal tapping would be done. She assured us that Dr. Parent and Dr. Graves did not think there would be any infection, but the procedure would be done later that week.

WEEK SIX: We went in for our regular visit to NICU and were told that Tyerria was doing well and that she would be going home tomorrow. We could not believe our ears. We were so happy. The nurse said Dr. Graves and Dr. Parent wanted to talk to us. She paged them both, but Dr. Graves was the only one that came. Dr. Parent called to have immediate surgery. Dr. Graves stated that Ty was finally 5 lbs. and 3 oz, the recommended weight for her to gain to go home. He told us she would go home tomorrow and asked if we were ready. We smiled and said yes. My heart was filled with so much joy that tears started to form. **HAPPY AND BLESSED TEARS!** I thanked God silently and tried to concentrate on what Dr. Graves told us. He told us to find a good pediatrician for her and that we would have to do follow-ups in a few weeks. He told us that his nurse and Dr. Parent's nurse would contact us to schedule appointments.

Dr. Graves explained that Tyerria would have this shunt in her brain for the rest of her life. He said, "We were hoping the swelling would decrease during the antibiotic treatments, but it did not. Also, she will need much physical therapy, and you must all do physical therapy at home. We must work on her movements to increase her motor skills, and Dr. Parent will explain all of that when we visit next week." To help, Dr. Grave stated that he would see Ty that same day to set up physical therapy to show us some home techniques to improve her motor skills. After that, he left us, and we left the hospital.

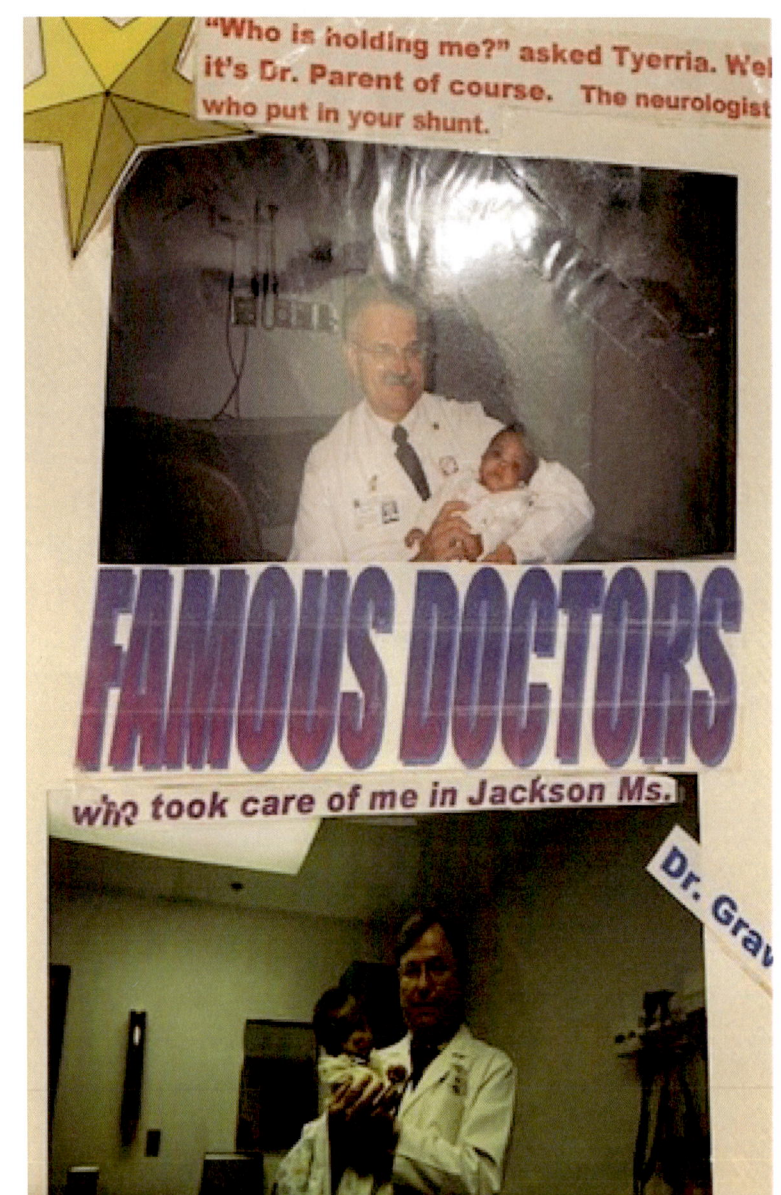

"Who is holding me?" asked Tyerria. Well it's Dr. Parent of course. The neurologist who put in your shunt.

FAMOUS DOCTORS

who took care of me in Jackson Ms.

Dr. Grav

Eleven
HOPE AND HEALING

Yes! Oh Boy! Smiling! Joyful! Happy! Loved!

I felt these things the next day after we visited with Dr. Graves. We did not even get a hotel room but stayed with our cousin Sean and his wife, Shontel (now divorced). We had become very close, and I feel that God brought us close because when they would visit us in Starkville with Uncle Bay and Aunt Lena Mae, we would talk but not too much. We just now had a strong bond and continues to be very close today.

Before going to Sean, we went and briefly talked to his brother Stanley at his house. Then, we returned to Sean's house and slept on an air mattress in his living room, which was a regular act since Ty had been sick. Once, we stayed at the Ronald McDonald house, but Terry preferred not to stay there because they assigned chores to do there. Terry did not like doing the chores that the manager assigned to each room, so we did not go back to stay again. I was tickled because our chores were to sweep the living area and the kitchen. A person would have thought they asked him to build the house; that was how bad he went about it. **Ronald McDonald House Charities of Mississippi (RMHC MS) serves as a "home away from home" for families**

of critically ill children who must travel to Jackson to receive intensive medical treatment (rmhcms.org., 2020).

This was why we started spending the night at Sean's house; his generosity saved us a lot of hotel money. We knew we would be taking Ty home the next day, so we did not want to go back home to Starkville, which is 2 1/2 hours away, and then try to come the next morning at 8:00 A.M. the next day. So, we stayed one more night at Sean's house. The night seemed long and drawn out, and it looked like it took forever for daylight to come. Finally, it was the morning of the 11th of August, which was my due date, or at least around that timeframe. Terry and I got up around 6:00 A.M., did our hygiene, thanked Sean, and headed toward University Medical Center Hospital. Sean told us that he and Stan would meet us up there to see Tyerria. So, we told them OKAY, hugged him, and could not thank him enough for all his help and letting us crash at his house. As Terry drove, I reflected on my delivery up to where I was at this point. I was so grateful to God and felt so blessed and could not wait to get our baby home. Terry parked the car in the parking garage, got out, got the car seat out of the back, and headed toward the hospital entrance. As we walked, all we could do was smile, and we took an elevator to the 2nd floor, which we could find the way to with blindfolds on. When we got to the

2nd floor, we were met by the nurse, who told us that we had to wash but only put gloves on, and Ty was wrapped up and ready to go. She asked me did I wanted to carry my little girl down, and if I would like, she would push me in a wheelchair. I told them we were fine, brought the car seat to strap her in, and Terry would take her down. At this time, the nurse got Ty out of her crib, where she was still so tiny, and most of her hair was shaved off. She looked like a little bright big-eyed bug that seemed to be taking everything in all her surroundings and voices. She was wide-eyed ready to say, "Hi, Mommy and Daddy." When Ty was strapped in her car seat, Sean and Stan came to see her and played with her some, and we headed out the door. We thanked all the nursing staff and told them to thank Dr. Graves and Dr. Parent for us. We left, headed toward the elevator, waited until it opened, and entered it. When we reached the first floor, Terry told me to wait until he got the car. As he left, he thanked Sean and Stan, gave them handshakes, and left to get the car. While Terry was going, we made small talk, and I thanked them and told them that this was not the last time because she would be back up for regularly coming back to Jackson for therapy and doctor visits. I hugged them as I saw Terry pull up, he got Ty, scrapped her in, and I got in the backseat to ride with her. We said goodbye to Sean and Stan and returned to Starkville with our baby girl.

Tyerria was so alert and did not sleep the entire ride home. She was looking around, and I played with her. At that moment, I got nervous because the thought of being a mom was finally kicking it, and I did not know what that consisted of. I tried to take my mind off this thought and looked in her diaper bag at the paperwork the nurse gave us. She left some specific instructions, which I was glad about. She told us that they fed her every three hours but not to rush things because she was still having problems sucking. The instructions said to constantly put our pinky in her mouth every two to three hours and push down on her tongue to help increase her sucking abilities, which was part of her therapy. We knew exactly what to do because we were briefed on it before we left and shown the proper way to do this. Also, in the paperwork, there were her appointment dates and times for each doctor and location, which was in the children's ward of the University Medical Center Hospital. Ty had an appointment on Tuesday at 10:00 A.M. and then at 11: A.M. with both doctors on the same day. After reading the instructions, I looked at some of the other materials she placed there on Hydrocephalus. I unfolded, read, and returned them to the bag. Finally, we were in Starkville and headed home. When we arrived home, it seemed like a parade because everyone was there. My family and his family lived near us except my brother Timothy, who lived in Minnesota, and my sister Willyne, who lived in Florida. They were all smiling and jumping up and down as we parked. We were bombarded in the car with family, and I loved it. This day was long overdue, and these are the ones that helped us pull through this. When we got out, we were crying, but they were tears of joy as we got out and walked into our house with our **MIRACLE BABY.**

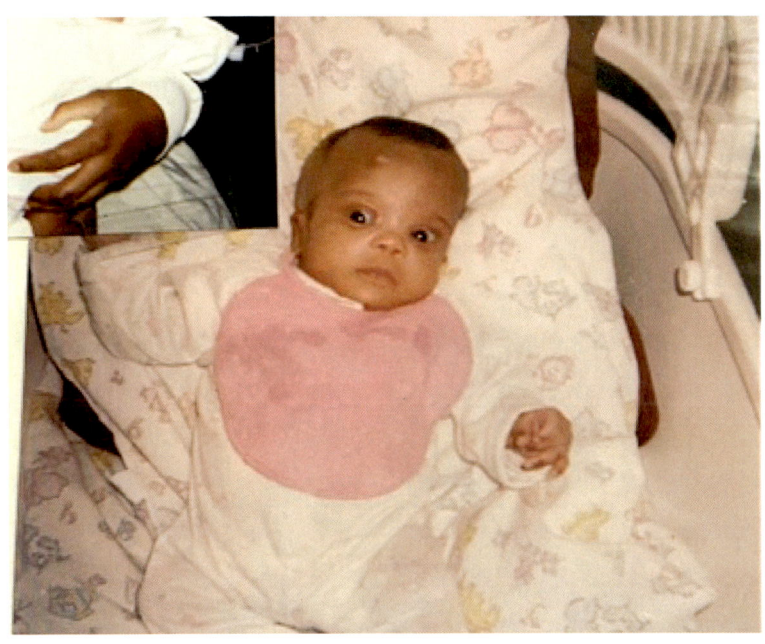

About three days later, we had to take Tyerria back to Jackson for her doctor's appointment. We went to the neurologist first-Dr. Parent. We checked in at the UMMC Children's Hospital, got our free parking pass, and went to the waiting room. After I checked in, we sat down, and I started to look around. I was shocked, amazed, hurt, heartbroken, and blessed. I was shocked and surprised because there were so many children with Hydrocephalus. The hurtful part was that their heads were shaped like a basketball, flat like a pancake or a football. It was so hurtful to see children like this. I had no idea, and I was heartbroken knowing that there were people scared like me. We did not know anything about this disability nor the long-term effects that it would have on children. I was blessed because Tyerria's head was almost normal, which was due to my sister Jeanette because she would come and shape her head when she visited. Anyway, I was relieved that Tyerria's head was not shaped like that and thankful to Jeanette for shaping her head. After about 10 minutes, Dr. Parent greeted all the children and parents. He was a tall man with a thick bushy mustache, and he greeted all of us and touched all the children's hands. Immediately, I fell in love with Dr. Parent's sincerity and concern for our children. We all could feel that he cared for the children, not just his job or the paycheck. Dr. Parent did this with each visit, and I was so happy because the children knew him well and fell in love with him. When we returned, the nurse assigned us a room and took Ty's vital signs. Then, she measured the circumference of her head and told us that she was in the 16th percentile of the head circumference of normal children her age. We were happy to hear this. She left us, and a few minutes later, Dr. Parent walked in and played with Ty for a little while. Then, he asked if he could walk around the waiting room to see Tyerria, offer them hope, and let them know that their child could also be in the normal range. We told him yes, and he went out, walking around the waiting room. Then, Dr. Parent returned and told us that Tyerria was doing good, but we had to do more. He told us that when we got to Dr. Graves, the pediatric doctor would set her up some therapy sessions. However, he told us it was not enough, and we had to do hours of therapy at home, which would be very intense. Dr. Parent said, "Mom, I do not care if you must cry while doing therapy-cry because it will look like you are abusing her, but I promise you that is not the case. I want you to trust me and continue the therapy even if she is crying, do not stop because so many moms stop because their child cries, and so they stop the therapy at home, and when they do, their child will remain handicapped and will have to depend on them for the rest of their lives. Mom and Dad, you must do this every day." We both agreed and then he finished Tyerria's checkup by feeling the bulb in her head and the tube running down her neck. He assured us that everything looked good and sent us on our way.

After leaving Dr. Parent, we went to Dr. Graves's office. We took our seats, and in about a minute, our names were called. The nurse took us to our room, and she said that before Dr. Graves came, the physical therapist wanted to talk to us about setting up appointments and giving us some techniques to work on at home. She stated that the therapist wanted to go over the physical therapy routine that would be done during each visit. The nurse left, and the Physical Therapist walked in, handed us a folder with many papers, and walked us through the information in the folder. The information consisted of home exercises, recommended toys, physical therapy items to work with Ty on, and a monthly progression sheet to track the success she will make. She suggested that we make a daily calendar that will schedule different family members to do exercises each day because Tyerria would need constant therapy to help her get to a normal life. Although she had limited movements and inabilities, we had to work on fine and gross motor skills.

Motor skills: a learned ability to cause predetermined movement outcomes with maximum certainty. www.wikepedia.com, 2021.

Gross motor skills: movement of large muscles of the arms, legs, and torso. www.understood.org, 2021.

Fine motor skills: the ability to move using small muscles in our hands and wrist. www.understood.org, 2021.

The physical therapist told us they would assess her progress each visit. She asked us whether we had any questions, which we did not because Dr. Parent had told us what to expect. Before she left, she said, "Mom and Dad, I know it will be hard, but you all push and push her hard. If you need to cry, cry, but Mom and Dad do not let up. I promise you. You will see the reward, and she will live a normal life. If you do not do this, she will be handicapped, and if you are like me, I want my child to be as normal as possible. You all can do this." She smiled and walked out of the room. About five minutes later, Dr. Graves walked in and examined Tyerria, reiterating what the Physical Therapist told us. He asked us if we had a pediatric doctor in mind at home, and I told him we did. He instructed us to take our paperwork there to inform them about Ty's disability. He told us to make sure we get her immunizations there as well. He finished and said to us that he would see us next week. We walked out, went to the receptionist, and made our next appointment.

These appointments went on like this every week. I made a calendar with family members on specific days to help with therapy. We bought every toy that was suggested on the recommended list. We bought all name-brand toys and no generic ones because I was adamant that these were the toys that would help my baby girl. **HOME THERAPY:** The doctors were not exaggerating when they said that physical therapy would be hard because Tyerria whimpered, cried, and pleaded with her eyes, and I knew it was hurting her. However, I kept going and doing it like it was recommended for us to do.

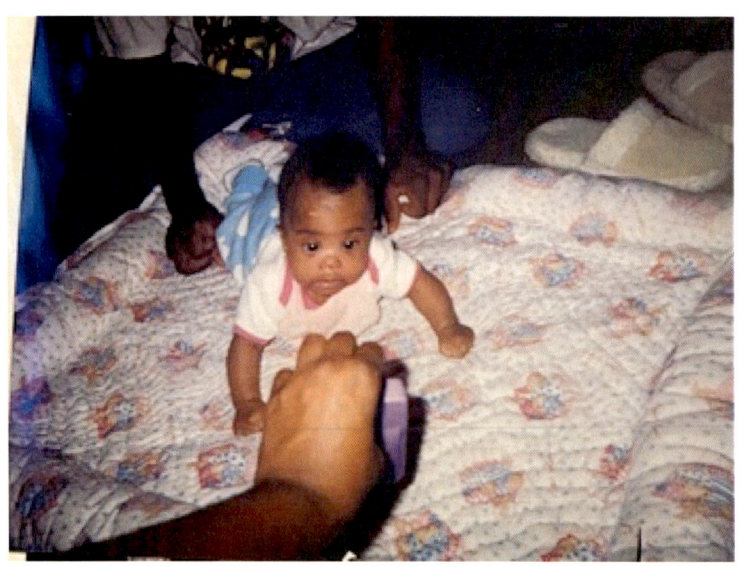

Ty-Ty, Asha an
Sanius (hey you can't h
Lisa)

See you can push up Ty-it
a matter of time(personal traine

gave specific instructions to my family, and they did exactly what I asked them to do. They cried but knew how important this was for Ty's health.

Therapy consisted of helping her learn to kick by pushing her knees hard on a toy that made a sound when she kicked it. We had to keep pushing her until she did it naturally. Next, we worked her tongue by pushing it up and down with our pinky finger so that the muscle would become stronger, and she could do such from a regular bottle nipple. After that, we took a ten-minute break but returned to work. We had to make her rollover by continuously pushing her hard to make her turnover. Then, we made her take the big toe in her hand and raise it to her mouth to suck her toes (this helped to improve flexibility). We also had to put her hand around a toy, help her squeeze it tightly, and then relax the grip. This was to help with her fine motor skills. This routine continued until she mastered those, then we were on to another set of therapy techniques, which started to get harder as she grew, and the months passed. We had to put her on all fours on the floor to help her learn to crawl. This was the one that broke my heart so much because her knees would buckle and give out, and she would lay flat on her stomach and cry. Her arms and legs were so small, and she would shake so badly, but we kept at it until her muscles were stronger enough to hold herself up. After this, it became more about helping her learn to walk and so much more.

During this process, things between Terry and me started to get worse, and we could not continue to be married any longer. This was when Tyerria was three months old. Before Tyerria was born, our marriage suffered, and we always fussed and fought. When I got pregnant with Ty, we stopped arguing all the time, but after that was over, and it seemed like Ty was in the clear, the fussing started back, and I could not take this any longer. I reached the point in life where I had to be there for my daughter, and I had to let Terry go. I could not allow myself to run or fight with him about the things he was doing. Although I never caught Terry, he was never home, which anyone would have thought would be due to Tyerria's disability. I knew that I was the one that carried her and gave birth to her, so it was time for one of us to grow up because it seemed like after she was getting better, he started back to his old routine. I will not go any further in details, but I filed for divorce, and within three more months, our divorce was finalized when Tyerria was six months old.

Also, during this process, Tyerria was christened at church because I gave her back to Christ. Rev. Nelson Forrest did the ceremony at my home church, St. Stephen United Methodist Church.

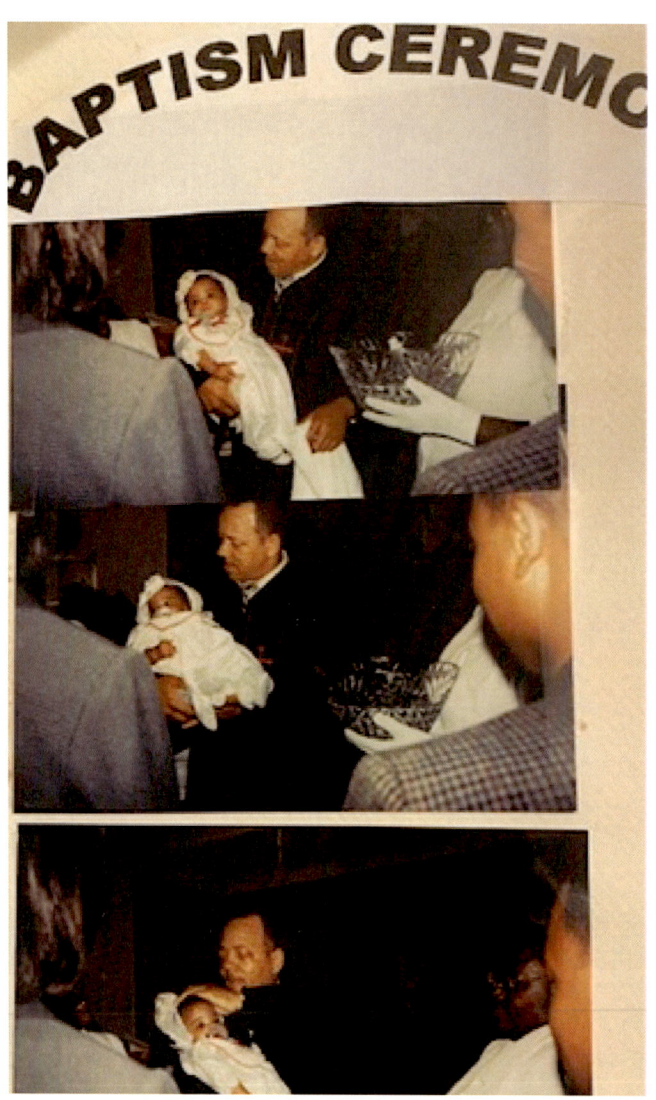

Our parents were there, and her God, parents-
Tony White and Vickie Walker (she is not a part
of our lives

anymore due to certain circumstances). However, I made another vow to my sister from another mother-Dorothy, Washington, which is now her Godmother since 2002.

Tyerria's therapy was still intense, and Terry did come over to do this part of home therapy and did attend therapy and doctor's appointments. After weeks of appointments, Ty's doctor visits turned into every three months, then six months visits, once a year, and finally, now every two years. I remember one incident when Tyerria was around seven months. The physical therapist looked for certain behaviors and movements that Ty should accomplish now. Ty had to pass different tests, and this one where we had to place a towel over her face, take her hand, and then make her pull it off her face. However, Terry did this as a peek-a-boo game by snatching the towel off her face, which she loved. Ty would laugh and kick her legs whenever he did this. When the physical therapist took her to the back to start her assessments, she immediately came back and got us and asked us to come to the back with her. My first reaction was that something was wrong with my baby, and we both asked simultaneously what was wrong. She told us that Ty did not pass one of the gross motor skills, and she was doing well until now. She told us to watch. She put the towel over Ty's face but did not reach for it. She said we had to redirect therapy and try something new to help her master this skill. Terry laughed and told her that he played a game with her, which he showed her. Tyerria was laughing and kicking all over the place. The therapist was relieved and said, "Dad, now I know you want to play peek-a-boo, but you cannot do it this way. She must pull the towel off her face." He told her that she would pull it off after about thirty seconds or less, which she did, and the therapist said that she needed to learn to pull it immediately but was pleased because she was in a normal range with her peers.

Each year, Ty went to see Dr. Parent. He would walk around with her to show other concerned parents that their child could do the same with hard work and intense therapy. After this comfort mechanism, he had the pleasure of doing a spinal tap on Ty to check the cerebrospinal fluid in the bulb inside her brain to check for infection. I am so glad that everything went well, which continued each year. Ty was improving and growing so much. She even got potty trained and was walking within her normal age group (at the beginning, she was diagnosed not to walk or be potty trained until she was four years old). **WON'T GOD DO IT! THANK YOU, LORD! THANK YOU, GOD! I WANT TO THANK YOU, LORD!**

However, in March 2008, Tyerria came home from school and started having bad headaches and was throwing up all over the house. I noticed her chest had a pocket-like bubble, which looked like a mass. I took her to the emergency room at Oktibbeha County Hospital, where they told me that I had to go to Jackson because the X-rays showed that the line connected to her shunt had broken in the area where the mass was in her chest. This was the building up of cerebrospinal fluid in her chest, and the University Medical Center would know what to do, and they have the equipment to handle cases like this. So, I drove down there with my sister Renee, and Terry met us there because he lives in Jackson, Mississippi.

When we arrived, it took them forever to call us back. The nurse told us she had to call Dr. Parent to inform him about Ty's X-ray. Shortly afterward, the nurse told us that Dr. Parent ordered an MRI to determine exactly where the break was and if she would have to go into surgery. Tyerria was eight years old and was afraid, but I told her that she was brave and that they would take pictures of the inside of her body, but she had to lay still. She asked the nurse if she could go to sleep and, when it was over, if she could see the pictures of the inside of her body. The nurse laughed and told her she would ensure she saw the pictures. Ty turned and looked at me and said, " Okay, Mommy, " Dr. Parent asked me if I liked taking pictures, and I said yes. He told me that the big machine would take pictures only inside the body. So, I am not scared anymore." I was shocked and relieved that she would do it without being afraid.

About an hour later, the technician came and got Ty and told us that it would only take about 10-15 minutes to conduct the MRI and that he would bring her back.

When the result was in, Dr. Parent informed us that Ty had to have surgery in a few hours to replace the tube lining in her body. He told us that he would have to shave part of her head again and maybe replace the bulb if it was not intact. When he left out, the nurse came back in with an assigned room for Ty and said that she would be staying in the hospital for a few days.

It was about 7:00 A.M. on a Wednesday. I called the school and worked to let them know what was going on. I called and told my family and Terry's family. For some reason, I was not afraid or nervous because I knew that God told me she would be fine and healed. However, Terry was a wreck, crying hard and apologizing for not being there. I assured him that this happened at school. A little boy threw Ty the basketball during Physical Education class, which hit her in the chest and caused the breakage. Around 9:00 A.M., my family and Terry's family were there, and they had already come to get Ty for surgery. I was calm, but Terry still was not, and I tried to talk him down. It took a while, but he did calm down. I asked him did he wanted anything to eat, but he said he was not hungry, but I was. I went down and got some Kentucky

Fried Chicken, and when I got back, his mom looked at me like I was crazy and asked me how I could eat. I told her that God told me she would be fine and that I needed to eat to get my strength up. She just looked at me, and then the nurse called and said they started the procedure and would give us updates every 30 minutes. Two hours later, the nurse called and said Ty did good and that everything went well. She said Dr. Parent put thicker tubing in but did not have to have the complete brain surgery because the old bulb was working correctly, so he attached the new tubing to the old bulb. Dr. Parent called and told us that he could not remove the old tubing because it was too deep, and he did not want to hurt her by cutting her in different places. He assured us that the old tubing would not hurt her. After I hung up, I told everyone what Dr. Parent told me, and we all praised God.

About 45 minutes later, the nurses brought Ty back to her room. My baby looked like the little boy on Karate Kid. The back side of her head was shaved off, and the left and front sides hung long and beautifully. My baby girl was so strong and endured so much. I am so blessed beyond anything.

Chapter Twelve
HOPE FAST-TRACK

Hope for a bright Future! Hope for Growing! Hope for love and Support from God and Family!
From 8-24 years old.

After the replacement, Tyerria has not had another revision or replacement shunt, which is rare according to medical evidence. The Hydrocephalus Associated states, "It is not uncommon for a person with Hydrocephalus to have ten to more shunt-related brain surgeries throughout their lifetime, and some individuals will undergo more than 100 surgical procedures (www.globenewswire.com). Thank you, God, for wrapping your arms around my child. Tyerria did not have to wear any helmets or disability devices despite what her regular pediatrician recommended for her to wear. I refused to let her wear these things because Dr. Parent and Dr. Graves told me not to and that she was normal, meaning she could play sports, run, climb, or do anything she wanted to do in life. She stayed on a constant average with her peers in school. Her growth, intellect, achievements, head circumference, movement, falling off things, getting back up, fighting with cousins, singing, but most

importantly, DANCING. She started dancing with KMG Creation under the leadership of Kalya Gilmore. Then, Tyerria joined the Academy of Performing Arts (ACPA) during elementary and high school because she loved dancing. She continued dancing until she graduated in 2017.

Tyerria Tanvzon Bryant

She even wanted to major in dancing and went to the University of Southern Mississippi to audition. Unfortunately, she did not make the dancing team, but that did not stop her.

Today, Tyerria is a vibrant, creative entrepreneur and proud graduate student. After she graduated from Starkville High School, she enrolled in Mississippi State University in August 2017. She graduated with a bachelor's degree in educational psychology in November 2020.

This year 2023, she received her master's in clinical Mental Health Counseling at the University of West Alabama.

She even wanted to major in dancing and went to the University of Southern Mississippi to audition. Unfortunately, she did not make the dancing team, but that did not stop her. Starkville High School, she enrolled in Mississippi State University in August 2017. She graduated with a bachelor's degree in educational psychology in November 2020. She is also the proud owner of Glossed by Tye, LLC, where she makes lip gloss, resin key chains, and eyelashes. Tyerria lives with her stepfather Dwayne Robinson, me, her mother-Terra, Robinson, and her adopted sister Luxury Wordlaw (my sister Renee's daughter). In December 2017, after Tyerria's college graduation, my loving, carefree, dancing-spirited sister, Renee Channel Wordlaw, was called home to Christ unexpectedly. She leaves her legacy, Tyerria's brother Lysanius (Aalecia)

Ford, and her grandchildren Khali, Kalyiah, Kylim, and Kaden. Because Lysanius was over 18, we could only adopt Luxury, but I am also present and there for my son and the kids. Tyerria and Saney have been close and have always called themselves brother and sister. She has two half-brothers, Cameron and Tyler (twins by her dad, and a sister-Grace), and Mariah and Chelisa-step sisters.

Her dad, Terry, is remarried to Kiesha and still lives in Jackson, MS. He is a constant in her life, and they have developed a strong relationship and continue to bond with him. He always takes them (her twins and her) out to eat. He constantly texts messages, inboxes (Messenger), pop-up visits, recitals, and other major events in her life and catches up on things happening in their life. When she was younger, she always visited Jackson on the weekends with her brothers. He is currently a truck driver.

Her stepfather, Dwayne, has been in her life since she was eight. We met when she was eight and have been together ever since. Despite his duties as a truck driver, he has taken her under his wing and been there for her for all her endeavors-dance recitals and other extracurricular activities or school programs. Today, Dwayne is now a Pastor and still there for Tyerria by giving advice, moving her into her dorm, then apartment, making corrections, and having small talks with her-etc.

Tyerria has an everlasting bond with her siblings and loves to laugh and visit them whenever possible. Her love for Luxury and Mariah is unbreakable. She is always there for them and helps me out amazingly with Luxury. Tyerria will be moving into her apartment and has started a new job at Community Counseling, working with Kindergartner through fifth-grade students. She has overcome any obstacles in her life, and by God's grace, she will continue to be strong and grow in her own life. I am incredibly proud of her and love her so much.

As for me-her mom-I thank God for her and His mercy and grace. God has given me a daughter that, with His love and blessing, helped her defeat the odds of being disabled from Hydrocephalus. God has planted some great people in her life that has helped her continuously grow, offer advice, and, most importantly, love her. As for me, I am a retired elementary school teacher of 25 years and retired in June 2023. I have over 20 years of experience as a Sergeant in the United State Army Reserves. I am a Pastor's Wife and a loving mother with a beautiful, loving family. I love my family and will be there for them, and I thank God for His blessing and my miracle baby-Tyerria Tanvzon Bryant.

PHOTOS OF TY AND FAMILY

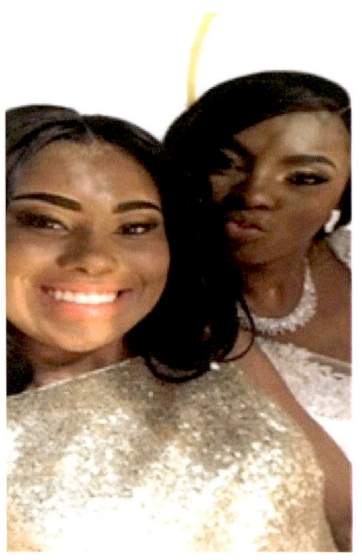

Auntee Jeanetter and Uncle JP

Ty Besties
Lyndrea

Bre

IN-LAWS

Dedication to my Jackson Family

Sean & Family

Stan & Family

Cousin Dee and Family
Dedication to my Jackson Family

Auntee Willyne

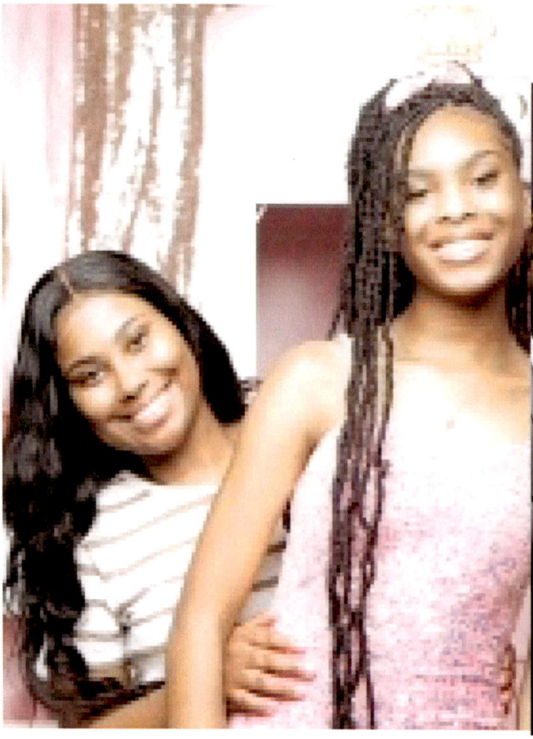

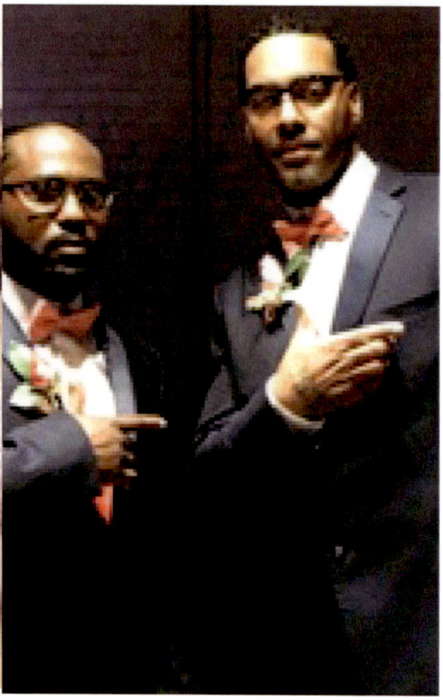

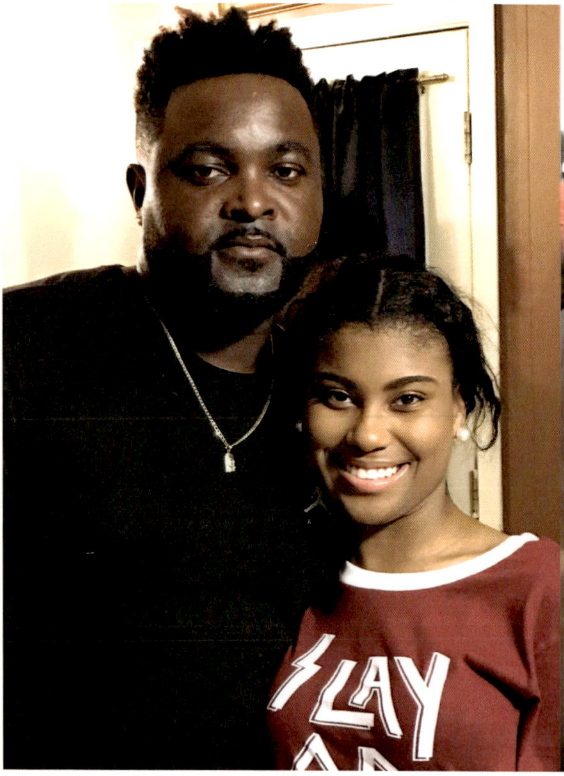
SLAY

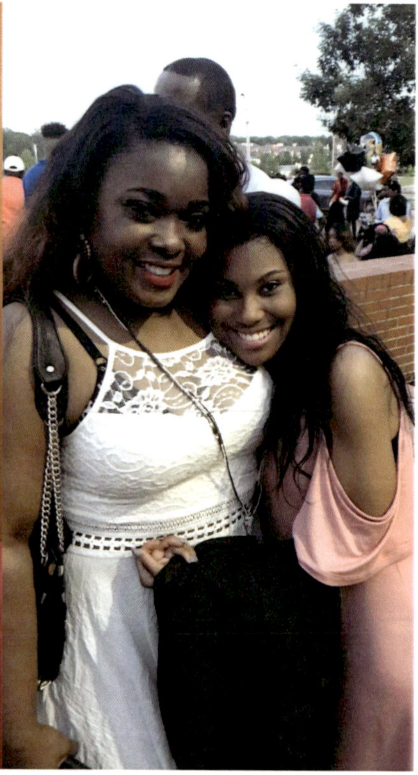

Tyerria TanV'zon Bryant
Our Miracle Child
May God's Grace continues to bless and
keep you. Love, Mom

In Memory: Grandpa Abe, Grandma Lou, Auntee Joyce & Auntee Renee-Rest in Love

Milton Keynes UK
Ingram Content Group UK Ltd.
UKRC032018120923
428570UK00005B/65